How to Get Big Things Done

So You Can Master the Universe

Andrew Soswa

Co-authors:

Alexander Castillo
David Gutowsky
Donna Kurtz
Ursula Skromblewicz
William Gaston

Copyright © 2020 Andrew Soswa

All rights reserved.

ISBN: 9781652493198

DEDICATION

To Alex, Iza, and all **kids who** keep learning to **become** smarter and kinder **future leaders**

CONTENTS

	Acknowledgments	i
1	Carrying the Team	1
2	We Can Do It Together	2
3	Break It Down	4
4	Is Making a Hot Dog a Project?	6
5	AWWW YEAH!	8
6	Keeping It 100 With the Squad	10
7	We Did It! Let's Have Fun Now!!	12
	About the Authors	14
	How this book was created	16
	Notes:	18

ACKNOWLEDGMENTS

Thanks to Donna, Alexander, Ursula, Bill and David.
Without them, this book could not happen.

1 CARRYING THE TEAM

Last summer Bob and his classmates went on a trip to the Walker Lake Campground in Wisconsin. Day one was half-way through when Mrs. Wilson suggested a tent setting activity. Bob grouped with Chris and Tommy as they hang out at school together.

They grabbed the closest tent bag and moved it towards a big tree. Bob pulled out the tent itself, tent poles, and stakes. There were two different size poles connected with bungee cords. The boys snapped them together. When they flattened out the tent, they crossed the long tent poles over it to form an "X" while passing through the flaps. They tried to place tips of the poles into eyelets at the end of the tent, but they were pretty hopeless. The tent kept plunging to the ground. They were getting frustrated when Bob got a simple idea.

Bob run for help to Mrs. Wilson. He received useful instructions. The boys positioned themselves at the tip of each pole to bend each pole in tandem and insert the tips into the eyelets. This way they raised the tent and secured it to the ground. Bob's quick thinking allowed them to complete the activity.

Rep:

This exercise gives participants the opportunity to experience a challenge in which the person that is elected the leader will work with the team to both help and lead the effort to problem-solve a situation that involves all of the participants and the leader.

Setting: Indoors or Outdoors

Space Requirement: Small Area

Group -Size: 8 - 12, ideally with a minimum of a least 4 participants to play.

Time to Conduct: 20 to 35 minutes

Instructions:

Have the group all face each other in a tight circle standing shoulder to shoulder. Have each person extend one hand into the circle and grasp the other person's hand from across the circle of you. Cross the other arm over their extended arm and reach for another person's hand across the circle. Ensure the two hands are holding do not belong to the same person. Now, the challenge is, become untangled without anyone letting go of the hands that they are holding onto. If the chain of hands is broken at any point, they must then start over again.

2 WE CAN DO IT TOGETHER

It was one of the last nice weekends of fall, and Mr. Adams took four kids from his young outdoor explorers' club camping. As the group approached the clearing at the end of the trail, they knew the campsite was near. Mr. Andrews asked the group to choose someone to be in charge of setting up the three tents that would be home for the group for the next two days. Donna said to the group that she goes camping all the time with her family, and she volunteers to help the group set up the campsite. The group agreed that Donna would be the best person to show them how to set up the tents for camping.

Donna picked out a location for the tents to be placed and set up. While the others were following Donna's instructions on how to set up the tents, Bill had walked off. Donna instructed Katie and David to work together while she goes to get Bill. Donna caught up to Bill and told him there would be plenty of time to explore. Donna told everyone that they had to work together to set up the campsite. After the campsite is set up, they would all go exploring the woods together.

Rep:

In this rep you're going to make your own chocolate banana bites. You can do it yourself but invite 2 of your friends to do it together. See what happens when you assign step 4 to one of your friends and steps 2 and 5 to the other one.

Ingredients:

- 2 ripe bananas
- A bottle of thick chocolate syrup
- Your favorite toppings like crushed peanuts or sprinkles

Be creative and replace sprinkles or crushed peanuts with your own unique toping like crushed candies. Want to make sandwich banana bites? Will a marshmallow hold two pieces of chocolate banana bites together? Together you can make this yummy snack faster, better and more creative way.

How to Get BIG Things Done

Steps:

1. Peal bananas and cut into 1-inch slices
2. Place banana slices onto a baking sheet lined with parchment paper
3. Chill banana bites for 30 minutes in a freezer
4. Use a fork to dip chilled bananas into the chocolate syrup one by one
5. Sprinkle the top with your favorite toppings
6. Set on a baking sheet and freeze until solid at least 2 hours

3 BREAK IT DOWN

Taylor was 12 and dreamed that when she was old enough, she would get a horse. Her parents said if she could show them how she could take care of a horse, and get her brother Jimmy involved, then they would help her to pay for it. Taylor and Jimmy began a plan to get their parents' support. They would write down everything to get a horse, take care of it, and have fun. As they started working on their list, they realized their friend Alex from 4H could help them since he and his sisters had two horses.

Taylor and Jimmy met with Alex, prepared with their questions, and came up with this plan:
1. Find a horse who is friendly, healthy, and energetic; and that Mom & Dad can afford.
2. Let the horse graze and provide supplements and water every day. Also, the horse needs to be brushed and washed 1-2x's per week, and the stable mucked out daily. Taylor and Jimmy will take turns each week to care for their horse.
3. Taylor and Jimmy will make a list with equipment and prices, so their parents understand the total investment.

Now, Taylor and Jimmy are ready to review this with their parents.

Rep:

Two to three friends or classmates come up with a plan on how they will achieve a dream that they share. First, this dream, such as getting on the Honor Roll, going to college, getting a summer job, getting shape, etc. is defined. Then they can break down the steps needed to achieve that dream so it can become a reality.

Look at the next page and complete the rep: Fill in these blanks to begin to break down the steps to achieve your dream.

How to Get BIG Things Done

1. In 1 to 2 sentences identify a dream that your team shares. Give enough detail as necessary so we really understand your dream.

   _____

   _____

2. How can you be a leader to achieve this dream?

   _____

   _____

3. Who do you want to work with to achieve your dream? How can you get them to share your dream too?

   _____

   _____

4. List all the people that you want to buy in to achieve this goal. Examples may include parents, potential employers, teachers, coaches, etc.

   _____

   _____

5. What lists will you and your team or teammate create to achieve this dream, so you know how to take the steps for your dream to happen?

   _____

   _____

4 IS MAKING A HOT DOG A PROJECT?

It is late summer, and Carlos is watching his favorite baseball team, the Chicago Cubs play, and Carlos is hungry. In particular, he has heard about this famous Chicago-style hot-dog and decides he wants one too to get the full experience of watching the Chicago Cubs.

Carlos is not sure if he has all the ingredients, but determined, he checks the fridge and finds out that he is missing hot dogs, buns, and a tomato. He is five minutes away from the store and decides he can get the ingredients quickly enough and not miss too much of his favorite team.

He rushes on his bicycle down to his local store and obtains the remaining items. Hurrying back, he gets busy with steaming the hot dog, getting all the ingredients out, slicing the tomatoes, and putting the hot-dog together. With it done in short-order, he is able to sit down to enjoy his tasty hot dog.

A project is a temporary endeavor undertaken to create something, like a unique product (hot dog), service (mowing the lawn), or result (a clean room). Carlos had an idea of what he wanted, a hot dog, he thought it through, make it into smaller steps, determined it could be done in the amount of time he desired, went out and did it, and then enjoyed the hot dog. Can you think of other things in life that are projects?

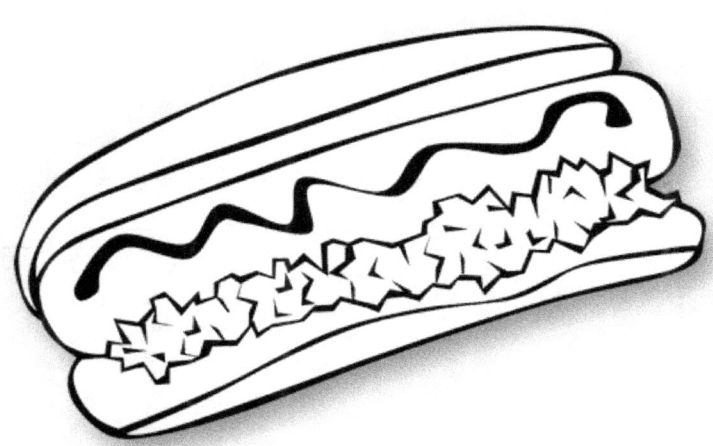

How to Get BIG Things Done

Rep:

In this rep you're going to have your team build a bridge by sticking to some rules below but also by encouraging them to be creative.

Build a marshmallow tower; team of 4-5

Supplies:
    20 spaghetti sticks per team
    One yard of string
    one yard of tape
    1 marshmallow

What's the tallest tower that you can make as team in 18 minutes? How about 6 minutes?

Your marshmallow must be on the very top, skewer it if you have to, but you can't eat it until the exercise is done.

You can't glue or attach, the structure to anything but itself (no propping it up with a selfie stick)

Try coming up with your own rules and goals. Are you bad enough to take several marshmallows and make free standing bridge? Want to make a phone stand? It's going be harder than you think to make someone's "easy" idea work.

No goal shaming, but firing shots is ok.

5 ...AWWW YEAH!

"I should go, and I don't not want to go. I Just wish that I wanted to go." Edd thought. He really wanted to audition at first but now it all just felt dumb and pointless, it was too much to bother with.

Edd always wanted to be a part of the school musical, he could sing, was popular and was a natural at presenting in English, but the only thing bigger than Edd's talent was his self-doubt. This was painfully obvious to his best friend Alex, who had encouraged him to audition for every performance in the past. So, he wanted to help his friend out and decided to forge Edd's signature on the audition waver.

Their music teacher was happy to call out Eddy's name to audition. Edd on the other hand was shocked to hear his name. With a nervous glance from Edd, Alex reassuringly shouted "AWWW YEAH!" Edd laughed, said "Awww yeah, I'm ready!" and finally auditioned on the spot. He got the lead role in West Side Story. He then went on to audition for the high school chorus group The Grape Jam.

10 years later, Edd is now an up and coming singer and composer.

Rep:

Let's play a game to get the excitement up.

Have all stand around each other in a group.

Have each person say "Look at me, I am a...." followed with by them mimicking an object or animal of their choosing and doing an action of that object or animal.

The rest of the persons then do the same thing that person did.

The next person, then says "Look at me, I am a...." followed with by them mimicking an object or animal of their choosing and doing an action of that object or animal, and then mimicking the previous person's action.

Example:

It starts off with "I am a chicken" followed by that person clucking like a chicken and flapping their arms in a wing flapping manner. Everyone then clucks like a chicken and flaps their wings. The next person then says "I am a cow" then moos like a cow, then flaps their arms like wings.

How to Get BIG Things Done

6 KEEPING IT 100 WITH THE SQUAD

The count is two outs, three balls, two strikes, and the score is Chicago Cubs three, and the Chicago Sox's zero with bases loaded, and the winning run at bat! The game rides on the shoulder of Elijah, the Cub's new left-handed pitcher. In past games, Coach Smith would typically have his son Tommy pitching, but something happened in practice earlier today.

Tommy is an okay pitcher, and the other players on the team knew that Tommy would always be the team pitcher because Coach Smith is his dad. Elijah pitched for the little league team where he uses to live. Elijah is a good pitcher and better than Tommy. The day of the big game and Tommy pitching was terrible in the pre-game practice. Something had to change if the Cubs wanted a chance at winning the championship.

After practice, the team had a meeting, Elijah raised his hand and said Coach Smith; you have always taught us to play as a team, win as a team, and we lose as a team, but Tommy's pitching is off today. I'm a good pitcher, and I want to help the team win. The next thing you know, the announcer says, "here's the pitch!"

Rep:
Follow the voice of the leader to retrieve and pop a balloon that is placed between the two-person team. You can up to 5 individual players playing.
Items:
- Blindfolds, Balloons, lots of open space

Setup:
- Each person will take a few balloons, blows them up, and place them in a bag.
- The group will choose someone to be the leader.

How to play:
1. The leader will choose two people, blindfold them, and interlock their arms while they stand back to back.
2. The leader moves a few feet away from the team and commands the team to walk towards the leader's voice.
3. When the team gets close enough to the leader, the leader will place a balloon between the team's backs.
4. The team has to pop the balloon without touching it while the team's arms are still locked together.
5. After popping the balloon, a new leader and team are chosen, and the game is repeated.

How to Get BIG Things Done

7 WE DID IT! LET'S HAVE FUN NOW!

Amber and the team has been debating for several hours on which science experiment the team should do for the upcoming Science Fair, but there are so many experiments to choose from. At times, the debate was intense between the team members, as some had strong feelings towards their particular idea.

With a little leadership and facilitation from Amber, she helped by taking notes, asking the pros and cons of each experiment and reciting them back to the team, and hosting multiple votes until there was a consensus. After many hours of heavy debate, they had settled on an idea of what to do.

With the consensus around an idea for their science experiment behind them, Amber and the team is feeling accomplished, but tired. Riding on the good feelings, Amber and the team pull out some pizza rolls and breadsticks out of their freezer and celebrate their small win. There is much more to do, but for now, they celebrate their progress.

Rep:

Have fun celebrating your accomplishments with a potluck party. What's a potluck? A partly to which each guest contributes a different dish to be shared.

Group size: limited only by the capacity of your party's location. Indoor or outdoor activity. Involves active participation of each guest. One person creates a list of participants with the name of the dish to bring and talks with others to find the best place for the party.

Each guest brings one dish and a piece of decoration. If there are more than 5 participants, one person may volunteer to bring just decorations and another to bring plates, cups and utensils if needed.

Items:

- Balloons, banners, confetti, flags, garlands, centerpieces
- A paper table cover, plastic utensils, cups and paper plates

Examples of potluck dishes: pizza, sandwiches, muffins, cookies, banana bites, chicken nuggets, hot dogs, mini burgers, sodas and water. Decorate your party place, play your favorite music and enjoy. You did it! Have fun now!

How to Get BIG Things Done

Celebrating Success After the Food Drive Project

ABOUT THE AUTHORS

Alexander Castillo is an upstart with 4 years of SAS and HAS solutions deployment and team management, he is currently pursuing his first Agile/PMP certifications. Motivated by a curiosity of technology and a desire to help others Alexander joined this project to gain experience while producing something of benefit to other people in with his background and beyond. Alexander enjoys Godzilla movies, Yo-Yos and solutions implementation.

Andrew Soswa is an accomplished coach and trainer with over 20 years in leadership and project management roles. His passion is to help others develop leadership and organizational skills.

Bill Gaston is a recently certified Scrum Master and aspiring Project Manager with over 25 years of IT experience. He desires to help others learn about a career in the Agile framework and profession in Project Management. Bill took the opportunity to work on the YPM project to learn more about Agile/Scrum and Project Management.

David Gutowsky is an IT professional, project manager, husband, and lives in Woodstock, Illinois with his wife and his family on a hobby farm. David is a graduate of Purdue University and has a Master's in Business Administration from Western Governors University. In his free time, David likes to run, bike, play with his dogs, and fight for Internet Freedom.

Donna Kurtz has over 25 years of experience in leadership and project management. As a teacher she has professionally taught children and adults in areas that encompass areas as diverse as tennis and education and is a Ph.D. candidate in Instructional Technology at Northern Illinois University. Donna believes deeply that leadership guidance and training taught at an early age can positively change young lives and foster greater contributions to their world.

Ursula Skromblewicz is an aspiring Project Manager particularly interested in the implementation of Agile values and principles. She was drawn to the project by curiosity of creating a unique product. YPM allowed her to learn while providing a source of knowledge to others.

HOW THIS BOOK WAS CREATED

1. Have a vision to help others

2. Design a persona for whom you are creating the book

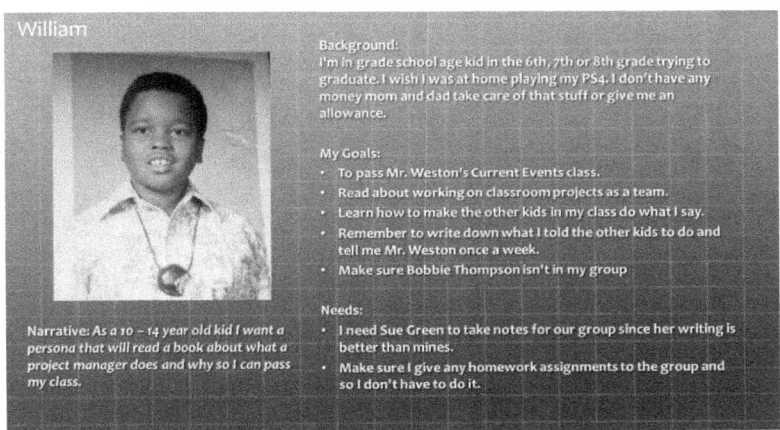

3. Design book's structure

4. Create chapters' titles

5. Write a story, activity, and add pictures for each chapter

6. Perform final edit

7. Publish it!

8. Celebrate success with the team!

Notes:

www.ingramcontent.com/pod-product-compliance
Lightning Source LLC
Chambersburg PA
CBHW070915220526
45466CB00005B/2224